from SEA TO SHINING SEA
MAINE

By Dennis Brindell Fradin

CONSULTANTS

Joel Webb Eastman, Ph.D., Professor of History, University of Southern Maine

Robert L. Hillerich, Ph.D., Professor Emeritus, Bowling Green State University; Consultant, Pinellas County Schools, Florida

CHILDREN'S PRESS
A Division of Grolier Publishing
New York London Hong Kong Sydney
Danbury, Connecticut

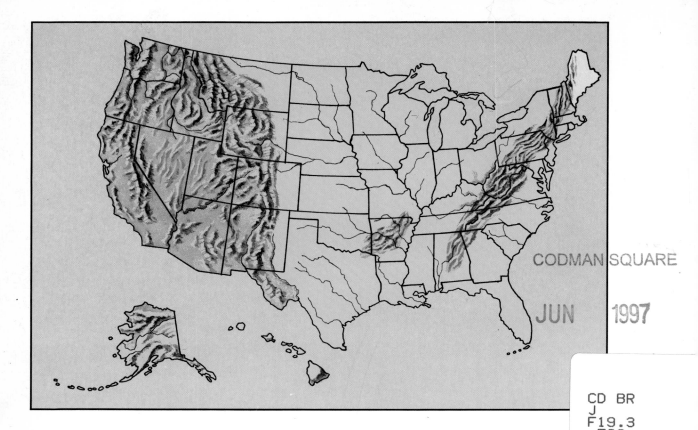

Maine is one of the six states in the region called New England. The other New England states are Connecticut, Massachusetts, New Hampshire, Rhode Island, and Vermont.

For my brother-in-law, Richard Bloom

Front cover picture: Pemaquid Point Light with tidal pool reflection; page 1, Boats at sunrise, Camden; back cover, Mt. Katahdin from Togue Pond, Baxter State Park

Project Editor: Joan Downing
Design Director: Karen Kohn
Typesetting: Graphic Connections, Inc.
Engraving: Liberty Photoengraving

Library of Congress Cataloging-in-Publication Data

Fradin, Dennis B.
  Maine / by Dennis Brindell Fradin.
    p.   cm. — (From sea to shining sea)
  Includes index.
  ISBN 0-516-03819-2
  1. Maine—Juvenile literature. [1. Maine.] I. Title.
II. Series: Fradin, Dennis B. From sea to shining sea.
F19.3.F68   1994   93-32680
974.1—dc20   CIP
                                          AC

Table of Contents

*Children playing at
Sand Beach, Acadia
National Park*

Introducing the Pine Tree State

Maine rises like a thumb in the northeastern corner of the United States. Each day, Mainers are the first Americans to see the sun. That is because Maine has the country's easternmost point.

Maine has played an important part in United States history. England's first northern colony was in Maine (1607-1608). The Revolutionary War's first sea battle took place there. In 1820, Mainers chose *Dirigo* as the state motto. It means "I lead."

Maine's nickname is the "Pine Tree State." Maine is a big maker of paper and lumber. It is also a leading grower of potatoes. Mainers catch most of the country's lobsters. Each year, many visitors enjoy Maine's rocky coast and small villages.

The Pine Tree State is special in other ways. Where were writer Stephen King and runner Joan Benoit Samuelson born? Where was the country's first blackboard made? Where were earmuffs invented? What state makes the most toothpicks? The answer to these questions is: Maine!

Overleaf: Fall foliage along Upper Togue Pond, near Baxter State Park

A picture map of Maine

Rocky Coast and
Pine Tree Forests

ROCKY COAST AND PINE TREE FORESTS

Maine is the largest of the six New England states. However, Maine itself is small. It covers only 33,215 square miles. Of the forty-nine other states, only eleven are smaller.

Maine is the only state that borders just one other state. That state is New Hampshire, to the west. Another country, Canada, borders Maine on the east, north, and northwest. The Atlantic Ocean is to the south and east.

Plant life on Cadillac Mountain

Tall mountains tower over Maine's middle and western parts. More than 100 mountains at least 3,000 feet high rise above Maine. Mount Katahdin is the state's tallest peak. It rises 5,267 feet above sea level. That is nearly 1 mile high. Most Maine mountains look green all year. They are covered with evergreen trees.

Deep, rich farmland lies in the middle of Maine. This land runs from northeast to southwest.

To the east, Maine's coastline stretches 228 miles. Its bays and harbors are good for shipping. The southern coastline has sandy beaches. Rocky cliffs line most of the coast.

TOPOGRAPHY

	100 m. 328 ft.	200 m. 656 ft.	500 m. 1,640 ft.	1,000 m. 3,281 ft.	2,000 m. 6,562 ft.	5,000 m. 16,404 ft.
Below Sea Level						

About 2,000 islands are also part of Maine. The largest is Mount Desert Island. It covers about 150 square miles.

Left: The moon over Schoodic Point, Acadia National Park

WOODS AND WILDLIFE

Nine-tenths of Maine is covered with forests. That is the largest rate of woodlands among the fifty states. Birches, maples, and oaks grow in Maine. Spruce and fir are among its many pine trees. The white pine is the state tree. The state flower is the white pine cone and tassel.

About 25,000 moose live in Maine. These animals weigh about 1,500 pounds each. The moose is

Most states are less than half wooded.

9

A moose and a pine tree are pictured on Maine's flag.

Sea gulls live along the Maine coast.

the state animal. Black bears and white-tailed deer are also found in Maine. Bobcats, foxes, beavers, and skunks live there, too.

Harbor seals love the rocky ledges along Maine's coast. Whales swim offshore in deeper water. Sea gulls and puffins live along Maine's coast. Chickadees live in the woods. The chickadee is the state bird.

LAKES AND RIVERS

The Pine Tree State has more than 2,500 lakes and ponds. Moosehead Lake is the biggest one. It covers about 120 square miles. No other lake completely within a New England state is as large.

More than 5,000 rivers and streams wind through Maine. The Androscoggin, Kennebec, Penobscot, and Machias are four major rivers. Many waterfalls are formed as they rush downhill to the sea. Two rivers form part of Maine's border with Canada. They are the St. John and the St. Croix.

CLIMATE

Maine is cooler than most other states. That is because it is so far north. On some summer days,

temperatures don't reach even 60 degrees Fahrenheit. People from warmer states visit Maine's cool woods each summer.

Autumn in Acadia National Park

Maine winters are snowy and cold. Winter temperatures can dip lower than minus 20 degrees Fahrenheit. About 7 feet of snow falls each year on Maine. Now and then, Maine has record cold spells. The year 1816 had one of them. Mainers called it "eighteen-hundred-and-froze-to-death."

FROM ANCIENT TIMES UNTIL TODAY

About 2 million years ago the Ice Age had begun. All of Maine was covered by glaciers. Much of Maine's coastland sank under their weight. Some hilltops became offshore islands. Glaciers also scooped out holes in the ground. As the glaciers melted, these holes filled with water. They became lakes.

Glaciers are huge sheets of slowly moving ice.

AMERICAN INDIANS

The Ice Age ended about 10,000 years ago. People reached Maine as the ice melted. These first Mainers were the ancestors of the American Indians.

About 5,000 years ago, the Indians developed a maritime culture. They lived along the ocean. These people dug clams and gathered oysters. The Indians ate the shellfish every season for thousands of years. They left behind huge mounds of shells.

One group of Indians lined the graves of their dead with red pigment. They are called the Red Paint People.

The American Indians had Maine to themselves for thousands of years. They picked berries and

Opposite: A 1909 picture of workmen at Percy & Small Shipyard, Bath

Maine's Algonquian Indians lived in dome-shaped wigwams like these.

hunted deer in the woods. They fished in Maine's rivers. Later, these Mainers grew corn and beans.

By the 1400s, several Algonquian Indian tribes lived in Maine. Place names show where they lived. The Passamaquoddy Indians lived around Passamaquoddy Bay. The Penobscot and Kennebec Indians lived along the rivers named for them.

EUROPEAN EXPLORERS

From about 1500 to 1600, England and France sent explorers to Maine. Some say English explorers coined the name *Maine*. It was short for mainland. Others claim that the French named the area. A part of France was once called *Maine*.

ENGLISH SETTLEMENTS IN MAINE

During the 1600s, England settled what is now the eastern United States. In 1607, Englishmen John Popham and Ferdinando Gorges sent colonists to Maine. In August, the colonists reached the coast. They began the Popham colony. It was founded where the Kennebec River empties into the ocean.

The settlers built houses and storehouses. They also built the *Virginia*. This was the first English ship built in North America. But the colony did not last. A bitter Maine winter and Indian troubles drove the colonists out. In 1608, they went back to England.

In 1620, the Pilgrims founded Plymouth, Massachusetts. Soon after that, English people again settled in Maine. The town of Saco was begun in 1623. Augusta started out as a trading post in 1628. Portland dates from 1633. By 1640, about 1,000 people lived in Maine.

Maine's first towns lay along the coast. Many of the settlers fished. Others trapped animals. Some traded with the Indians for furs. Maine's forests gave rise to the lumber industry. New England's first sawmill was built in Maine in 1631. Maine provided many pine trees for ship masts. It was called the "Mast Country."

John Popham, sponsor of the Popham colony

John Winter founded one of Maine's first ship-yards around 1637. Maine became a major ship-building center. Maine-built ships carried fish, furs, lumber, and masts to England.

As settlers moved inland, farming gained importance. Corn was the main crop. Many families ate corn at nearly every meal. They raised cows for milk and butter. They hunted deer and other animals for meat.

Maine did not have a large population. Its government was weak. By 1658, Maine's colonists decided to become part of Massachusetts. In 1677, Massachusetts bought Maine from the Gorges family. For nearly 150 years, Maine remained part of Massachusetts.

THE FRENCH AND INDIAN WARS

Between 1689 and 1763, France and England fought over North America. In the United States, these were called the French and Indian Wars. Many Indians helped the French. France ruled Canada at that time. Canada borders all of northern Maine. That is why much fighting took place in Maine. The Indians burned many towns. But English Mainers kept rebuilding.

Thousands of Mainers fought France. Two Mainers became heroes. In 1690, William Phipps of Woolwich led a fleet with 700 men. They gained Nova Scotia, Canada, for England. In 1745, William Pepperrell of Kittery led a fleet to northeast Nova Scotia. His forces took the great French fort at Louisbourg.

In 1755, the English removed French settlers from Nova Scotia. They were known as French Acadians. Many of them later settled in northern Maine.

Finally, in 1763, the French and Indian Wars ended. France lost all of its land in North America. England was now master of North America.

During the French and Indian War, William Pepperrell (above) and his forces took the French fort at Louisbourg (below).

THE REVOLUTIONARY WAR

By 1764, Maine was doing well. The colony had 25,000 settlers and nearly fifty towns. Each year, Maine shipped millions of pounds of fish and lumber. But England was in debt. The government had borrowed money for the French and Indian Wars. To pay off the loans, England placed more taxes on the Americans.

Each year, Mainers honor the beginning of the Revolutionary War on Patriots' Day. It is celebrated on the third Monday in April.

One of the English taxes was on tea. In 1774, patriots in York, Maine, burned English tea. This is called the "York Tea Party." On April 19, 1775, the Revolutionary War (1775-1783) began in Massachusetts. The Americans fought to break free from England.

The first sea battle of the war occurred in Maine. On June 12, 1775, patriots in Machias rowed out into the harbor. They attacked the English ship *Margaretta*. After its captain was shot, the *Margaretta* surrendered.

The first sea battle of the Revolutionary War took place in the harbor at Machias (above).

In October 1775, the English attacked Portland. They shelled the town from their ships. No townspeople were killed. But more than 400 buildings were destroyed.

Six thousand Mainers fought in the revolution. They took part in battles in New York and

Massachusetts. About 1,000 Mainers wintered with George Washington at Valley Forge. In 1783, a peace treaty recognized America's independence. About 1,000 Mainers died giving life to the United States.

In October 1775, the English shelled Falmouth (now the city of Portland). More than 400 buildings were burned.

STATEHOOD AND GROWTH

After the Revolutionary War, more people settled in Maine. By 1785, Mainers started asking for statehood. During the War of 1812 (1812-1815), the United States again fought England. The United States wanted freedom in trading and shipping. English troops landed in Maine. Maine's shipping

was hurt. Massachusetts did little to help Maine. In 1815, the United States won.

After the war, Mainers pushed harder for statehood. They wanted to be separate from Massachusetts. By 1820, nearly 300,000 people lived in Maine. That was more than enough for statehood. On March 15, 1820, Maine became the twenty-third state.

William King was Maine's first governor. Portland served as the first state capital. In 1832, Augusta became the capital. It was closer to the center of Maine's population. Augusta has been the capital ever since.

The capitol, in Augusta

Farming and industry continued to grow in the new state. By 1820, potatoes were replacing corn as the number-one crop. They grew well in the Aroostook, Kennebec, and Penobscot valleys.

Lumbering became the state's largest industry. Maine's shipyards used the wood to build some of the world's best cargo ships. Bath became America's leading shipbuilding city.

Bath was named for Bath, England.

One of New England's first railroads was built in Maine in 1836. It carried lumber in the Bangor area.

Mainers also made new products. The country's first blackboard was used in Rumford in 1816. In 1847, Hanson Gregory of Camden made the first doughnuts. In 1848, the first chewing gum was made in the United States. It came from Bangor. In 1873, Chester Greenwood of Farmington invented earmuffs. Later, he opened an earmuff factory. Farmington became the "Earmuff Capital of the World."

THE FIGHT AGAINST SLAVERY

Maine played a key role in the fight for the rights of black people. In 1802, Bowdoin College opened in Brunswick. Bowdoin admitted black students. It

Left: Harriet Beecher Stowe
Right: General Oliver Otis Howard

was one of the first United States colleges to do that. John Russwurm was Bowdoin's first black graduate (class of 1826). In 1827, he helped found *Freedom's Journal*. It was the country's first black-run newspaper.

Maine was admitted to the Union as a free state in 1820. No slavery was allowed there. Slavery was not allowed in the other northern states, either. The South, though, had huge numbers of black slaves. In 1834, the Maine Antislavery Society was formed in Augusta. The group worked to end slavery in the South. In 1852, Harriet Beecher Stowe's book *Uncle Tom's Cabin* was published. She wrote it in Brunswick. This novel told about the evils of slavery. Thousands of Americans read it.

Hannibal Hamlin was a great Maine lawmaker. In the 1850s, he helped form an antislavery party. It was called the Republican party. In 1860, the Republicans ran Abraham Lincoln for president. Hamlin ran for vice president. The pair won the election.

Soon after Lincoln and Hamlin took office, the Civil War (1861-1865) began. It was a fight between the North and the South. Slavery was a major cause of the war. About 73,000 Mainers served the North. Two of them became generals. General Oliver Otis Howard of Leeds lost his right arm. General Joshua Chamberlain of Brewer was

These Civil War soldiers from Maine fought for the North.

wounded several times. About 7,500 Mainers died in the war. In 1865, the war ended. The North had won. The northern victory freed the slaves.

RAILROADS AND FACTORIES

Meanwhile, Maine was growing. The late 1800s were big railroad-building years in the state. The Aroostook Railroad was finished in 1894. Trains helped Aroostook County farmers move their potatoes to market. Aroostook County became one of the world's great potato-growing areas. Maine factory goods were carried by train, too.

New industries grew in the state. Cloth making became important after the Civil War. So did the making of shoes. More trees were felled to make paper than for lumber. But Maine continued as a lumber and shipbuilding center. By 1900, half the ships in the United States had been built in Maine. By then, most of them were made of steel, however. The major new shipyard was the Bath Iron Works.

WARS AND DEPRESSION

In 1898, the United States fought and won the Spanish-American War. It started when the battle-

A Maine potato field in blossom

ship *Maine* was blown up in Havana, Cuba. About 2,000 Mainers served in that war.

World War I began in 1914. It was fought in Europe. The United States stayed out of the war until 1917. Before then, some Mainers joined Canada's armed forces. From 1917 to 1918, 35,000 Mainers served with the United States forces. Ships from Maine helped win the war.

In the 1920s, Aroostook County farms got larger. Growing potatoes, dairy farming, and raising chickens became big business. During those years, the paper industry boomed, too.

In 1929, Maine began ten years of hard times. This was called the Great Depression (1929-1939).

In long-ago days, teams of horses did much of the work at Maine shipyards.

Every state suffered from the hard times. Farms, factories, and banks failed in Maine.

World War II (1939-1945) helped end the Great Depression. The United States entered the war in 1941. During this war, about 95,000 Maine men and women served. More than 2,000 Mainers died for their country. Mainers at home built hundreds of ships and submarines. Maine's factories turned out uniforms and boots.

GROWTH, PROBLEMS, AND SOLUTIONS

During World War II, dozens of destroyers were built at the Bath Iron Works (above and below).

After the war, the country enjoyed a boom in tourism. Maine became a big vacationland. Hotels

and vacation cottages went up along Maine's lakes and seashore. Visitors also came for winter sports. Ski lodges were built in the mountains.

In the 1950s and 1960s, air-force bases were built. Electronics companies came to Maine. Paper and food-packaging companies grew.

Maine's Indians have not shared fairly in the state's wealth. In 1972, the Passamaquoddy and Penobscot Indians filed a lawsuit. They claimed that their land had been wrongly seized. They showed a 1794 treaty as proof. In 1980, the United States government agreed with their claim. The government paid the tribes $81.5 million for their land. Both tribes bought forestland. The Passamaquoddy also bought blueberry fields. Today, they are Maine's second-largest blueberry growers.

The early 1980s were good for Maine. The state's population grew by almost 10 percent. New businesses moved in. But in the late 1980s, a recession hit the Northeast. Businesses—both old and new—closed. Between 1989 and 1993, about 30,000 Mainers lost their jobs. By 1993, Maine had the country's third-highest jobless rate. The Lewiston-Auburn area was hard hit.

Pollution has also become a problem for Maine. By the 1980s, waste from cities was harming coastal

After World War II, Maine became a vacationland, even in winter.

A recession is a period of hard times. But it is less severe than a depression.

waters. Sea animals died as the water was poisoned. Casco Bay, at Portland, became badly polluted. Clams and cod in the bay died or became diseased.

Many Mainers want more done to protect their forests. Disease and overcutting of some woodlands have claimed millions of trees. During the 1980s, loggers built 11,000 miles of roads into the woods. Vacation homes went up along these roads.

Maine is dealing with its problems. In 1990, Casco Bay became part of the National Estuary Program. This program protects areas where rivers meet the sea. The same year, Maine and nearby

The manufacture of paper products is Maine's most important industry. This paper mill is in Bucksport.

states formed the Northern Forest Lands Council. It works to protect northeastern woodlands.

By 1994, Maine was recycling half of its wastes. This has helped reduce pollution. Maine is also working to tackle unemployment. In 1993, the Youth Apprenticeship Program started. It offers job training to young adults.

Maine's state motto, *Dirigo,* means "I lead." Mainers fought the first sea battle of the revolution. They led in the fight against slavery. Now, Maine hopes to lead the country into the year 2000.

Logging in Maine has claimed millions of trees.

Overleaf: A potato harvester in Aroostook County

Mainers and Their Work

MAINERS AND THEIR WORK

The Pine Tree State is home to about 1.2 million people. Only twelve states have fewer people. About 98 of every 100 Mainers are white. Their ancestors came from many lands. One-fourth of them trace their roots to France or French-speaking Canada. French is still spoken in many Maine households. Many Maine families came from England, Ireland, Scotland, Germany, Sweden, and Italy.

Only about 25,000 Mainers are Asian, Hispanic, American Indian, or black. They are divided rather evenly between the four groups.

Mainers are an outdoors people. They sail, swim, and fish in warm weather. Many like to hike and bicycle. In cold weather, Mainers ski and ice skate. Dogsled racing and hockey are other winter pastimes.

About 98 percent of Mainers are white, and about 25 percent of them have French ancestors.

Maine ranks high in ways that make life pleasant. Only thirty-seven people per square mile live in Maine. That makes Maine the least crowded of the eastern states. Maine also has one of the country's lowest crime rates.

Many states have low voter turnouts. But

Some Mainers are craftspeople. The boatbuilder shown here makes boats by hand. The weaver is making fabric on a loom.

Mainers treasure their voting rights. In 1992, Maine ranked first among the fifty states in voter turnout for the presidential election.

THEIR WORK

About 560,000 Mainers have jobs. Roughly 140,000 of them sell goods. Many salespeople work in Maine's thousands of tourist shops. They sell items such as T-shirts and mugs. Other Maine stores sell goods ranging from food to television sets. The L. L. Bean Company is based in Freeport. Mainer Leon Leonwood Bean founded this famous mail-order firm. The company sells boots, tents, and other outdoors goods.

Another 150,000 Mainers do service work. They include health workers, lawyers, and boat and car repairers. Maine's 95,000 government workers include letter carriers and teachers.

More than 100,000 Mainers make products. Paper goods are Maine's leading product. Toothpicks, clothespins, and matches are some of Maine's special wood products. Many Christmas trees come from Maine.

Maine is one of the leading shoe-making states. It is a big maker of clothing and other cloth goods.

*Lobster fishing off
Maine's rocky coast*

Boats and ships, computers, and packaged foods also come from Maine. Frozen french fries, lobsters, and blueberries are shipped across the country.

The Pine Tree State's 7,000 farms help feed the country. Maine is one of the top potato-growing states. Each year Maine grows about 3 billion pounds of potatoes. That is 12 pounds for each American. Milk and eggs are also important farm products. Maine ranks first in the country at growing blueberries. Peas, dry beans, apples, oats, and strawberries are other major crops.

Maine is a top fishing state. Nearly 90 percent of the country's lobsters come from Maine. Only Maryland leads Maine at harvesting soft-shell clams. Cod, flounder, and tuna are other big catches.

*Overleaf: The harbor
at Perkins Cove*

A Tour of the Pine Tree State

A TOUR OF THE PINE TREE STATE

Maine is a wonderful place to visit. The state has small but interesting cities. Many historic sites add to the state's charm. Few places can match the beauty of Maine's rocky coast, woods, and streams.

UP THE MAINE COAST

Most of Maine's major cities lie on or near its coast. Half of all Mainers live there.

Kittery is at the Maine-New Hampshire border. The oldest United States naval shipyard is there. The Portsmouth Naval Shipyard dates from 1800. It was named for the city of Portsmouth, New Hampshire, just across the Piscataqua River. Submarines are repaired and serviced at the shipyard.

York is just up the coast from Kittery. A famous jail is there. The Old Gaol was built in 1719. Today, visitors can enter the old cells. Now, the jail houses displays on York history rather than prisoners.

The Rachel Carson Wildlife Refuge is the next stop. Rachel Carson was an author. She wrote about the seashore and its wildlife. Deer and moose roam

Piscataqua River sunset, at Kittery

the refuge that was named for her. Birds seen there include owls and black ducks.

To the northeast lies a famous resort area. Mainers call it "the Kennebunks." Villages there include Kennebunk, Kennebunk Beach, and Kennebunkport. People sail in the ocean off the Kennebunks. Children play on the sandy beaches. Seals live along the offshore islands. Kennebunkport has become well known because former president George Bush has his vacation home there.

The Wedding Cake House stands in Kennebunk. It is decorated like a wedding cake. A sea captain had it built for his bride in 1826. He had

Left: The Wedding Cake House, in Kennebunk
Right: The Mousam River, near Kennebunkport

The Seashore Trolley Museum, in Kennebunkport

Wooden sailboats on Penobscot Bay

to leave for sea on their wedding day. They didn't even have time to eat their wedding cake.

Kennebunkport has the world's largest trolley collection. The Seashore Trolley Museum displays about 200 old streetcars. Visitors there can ride in some of the trolley cars.

Portland is north of Kennebunkport. With 64,358 people, Portland would be a small city in many states. But it is Maine's largest city. Nearby is South Portland. With about 23,000 people, it is Maine's fifth-biggest city.

Portland is known for shipping. Few East Coast cities have more ship traffic. Ships carry oil, fish, and

other goods in and out of the port. The oldest of Maine's sixty-two lighthouses is near Portland. Called Portland Head Light, it was completed in 1791. Many artists have painted Portland Head Light.

Poet Henry Wadsworth Longfellow was born in Portland. At his childhood home, visitors can see his writing desk. The Portland Museum of Art is another highlight of the city. Paintings by Maine artist Winslow Homer hang there.

Bath is up the coast from Portland. Bath was once the world's leading maker of wooden ships. Today, the Bath Iron Works builds ships for the United States navy. The Maine Maritime Museum is also in Bath. Displays there trace Maine shipbuilding back to the 1600s.

Rockland lies on the southern end of Penobscot Bay. That is about halfway up Maine's coast. The Shore Village Museum is in Rockland. It has the country's largest collection of lighthouse lenses. Children can climb inside one of them. They can also operate the lighthouse foghorn. Foghorns are used to warn ships of danger.

East of Penobscot Bay is Acadia National Park. It lies on part of Isle au Haut and Mount Desert Island. Acadia is New England's only national park.

A lighthouse is called a "light" for short.

Portland Head Light is Maine's oldest lighthouse.

Some lighthouse lenses can shine a light about 22 miles across the water.

Plants found in Acadia National Park include wild lupine (left) and blueberry bushes on Cadillac Mountain (right).

It is the oldest national park in the East. Acadia was set aside in 1916. The park is a place of woodlands, lakes, seashore, and mountains. The highest peak along the country's Atlantic coast is on Mount Desert Island. Cadillac Mountain stands 1,530 feet tall. Visitors can drive to the mountain's top.

Northeast of Acadia National Park, on the mainland, is Machias. The Burnham Tavern Museum is there. The tavern was built in 1770. American patriots met there in 1775. They planned the capture of the *Margaretta*. Today, museum visitors view displays of items from colonial times.

Farther northeast is Lubec. It is at Maine's southeast corner. Lubec is also the easternmost point of the United States. President Franklin D. Roosevelt vacationed nearby on Campobello Island. The island is east of Lubec. It is part of Canada. The Roosevelt Bridge links Lubec with the island. At Campobello, visitors can tour the grounds. They can also see Roosevelt's famous hat and walking sticks.

THE SOUTHERN INTERIOR

Bangor is Maine's third-biggest city. It has about 33,000 people. Paper is made in the Bangor area. Many people use Bangor as a stopping place. Then, they head farther inland to fish and hunt.

The Cole Land Transportation Museum is in Bangor. Displays there show how travel in Maine has changed. Old wagons, railroad cars, and children's buggies are on view. Old sleighs can be seen there, too. In the past, Mainers traveled over snow in horse-drawn sleighs.

South of Bangor is Augusta. Long ago, Indians held meetings there. They called it *Cushnoc*. The name may mean "sacred place." Today, Maine's lawmakers meet there in the state capitol. The

Roosevelt Bridge links the town of Lubec with Campobello Island.

building is made of granite from nearby Hallowell. A golden statue of a woman stands atop the 185-foot-high dome. She holds a pine bough. That is an emblem of the Pine Tree State.

Blaine House is near the capitol. This twenty-seven-room mansion serves as the governor's home. James G. Blaine once lived there. He was Speaker of the United States House of Representatives (1869-1875).

The Maine State Museum is also near the state capitol. Children enjoy the exhibit "12,000 Years in Maine." Relics dating back to the Ice Age are featured. The museum has other displays on Maine's people and industries.

Fort Western is another Augusta landmark. The fort was built in 1754. Part of the original fort still stands.

To the southwest are Maine's "Twin Cities." Lewiston and Auburn are on opposite banks of the Androscoggin River. Lewiston, on the east bank, has about 40,000 people. It is Maine's second-biggest city. Auburn, on the west bank, has about 24,000 people. It is Maine's fourth-biggest city. Lewiston is home to Bates College. It is New England's oldest college to enroll both men and women.

Students on the Bates College campus, in Lewiston

Northwest of the Twin Cities is Paris. Hannibal Hamlin was born there. His childhood home is not open to the public. Visitors can enter the Hamlin Memorial Library and Museum next door. It is inside an old jail.

North of Paris is Farmington. A one-room school there dates from 1852. Today, it is called the Red Schoolhouse Museum. Farmington holds Chester Greenwood Day each winter. The event was named for the inventor of earmuffs. There are snowshoe races and cross-country skiing races.

NORTHERN MAINE

Moosehead Lake is in northwest Maine. The lake is shaped like a moose's head, antlers and all. This part

Blaine House, in Augusta, is the governor's home.

of Maine is known for great hunting and fishing. Streams in the area attract canoeists and rafters.

Northern Maine is one of the country's top logging areas. The Lumberman's Museum is at Patten in northeast Maine. There, visitors can learn how logging has changed over the years. The museum's displays include a model of an 1820 logging camp.

Aroostook County is in northernmost Maine. New Englanders call it "The County." Aroostook County covers 6,453 square miles. Rhode Island and Connecticut could fit into the area. Aroostook County grows more potatoes than any other United States county. In the fall, the children help with the potato harvest. They are excused from school to do that.

Some people in Aroostook County are French Acadians. They read newspapers in French. Some listen to French radio shows from Canada. Their ancestors were pushed out of French-Canada by the British in 1755. Van Buren is an old French Acadian community. It is in far northeastern Maine. The Acadians settled this town on the St. John River in 1790. Acadian Historic Village is in Van Buren. Sixteen old buildings from around the area were moved there. They include houses, a school, a blacksmith shop, and a church. All belonged to

French Acadians. The buildings have been furnished to show how Maine's early French Acadians lived.

In western Aroostook County, the Allagash Wilderness Waterway winds northward. It consists of lakes, ponds, and rivers. This waterway is one of America's most beautiful and least spoiled places. Canoeists and hikers go there to test their skills.

Baxter State Park is near the waterway's southern end. It is Maine's largest park. The state's highest peak is inside the park. The Indians named it *Katahdin*. That means "high place." Trails lead to the top of Mount Katahdin. There, the sun can be seen as it first rises over the United States.

Farm fields in Aroostock County

Overleaf: Henry Wadsworth Longfellow

45

A Gallery of Famous Mainers

A Gallery of Famous Mainers

Dorothea Dix

Winslow Homer

Many famous people have lived in the Pine Tree State. They include government leaders, poets, and a long-distance runner.

Dorothea Dix (1802-1887) was born in Hampden. By the age of fourteen, she was teaching school in Massachusetts. Later, Dix helped start mental hospitals in several states. She also improved conditions in the country's prisons. During the Civil War, Dix headed the Union army's nurses.

Countless artists have painted pictures of the sea. **Winslow Homer** (1836-1910) was one of the best. Although he was born in Massachusetts, Homer later lived near Portland. *The Fog Warning* and *Mending the Nets* are two of his fine works.

Abbie Burgess (1839?-1892) was a lighthouse-keeper's daughter. In 1853, her family moved to an island. It was 25 miles from Rockland. There, Abbie helped her father run Matinicus Rock Light. She sometimes ran the lighthouse alone. Later, she married a lighthouse keeper and helped him, too.

Melville Fuller (1833-1910) was born in Augusta. After graduating from Bowdoin College,

Senator Margaret Chase Smith was the first woman to wage a major campaign for the office of President of the United States.

he became a noted lawyer. In 1888, he was named chief justice of the U.S. Supreme Court. Fuller headed the country's highest court for twenty-two years.

Gail Laughlin (1868-1952) was born in Robbinston. When she was twelve, she made herself a promise: to "study law and dedicate my life to the freeing of women." She kept her promise. Laughlin helped women gain the right to vote. She fought for women's rights in the workplace. She also served in the Maine legislature.

Margaret Chase Smith (1897-1995) taught in a one-room school in Skowhegan. That was her

birthplace. Later, she became one of the most popular lawmakers in Maine's history. She served in the U.S. House of Representatives (1940-1949). In 1948, she was elected to the U.S. Senate. She was the first woman elected to serve four terms there (1949-1973). In 1964, she waged a major campaign for president. She was the first woman to do that.

Nelson Rockefeller (1908-1979) was born in Bar Harbor. He also became a politician. He served as governor of New York (1959-1973). Rockefeller then served as vice president of the United States (1974-1977).

Edmund Muskie was born in Rumford in 1914. He was Maine's governor from 1955 to

Senator Edmund Muskie

1959. Muskie tackled his state's pollution and education problems. In 1958, Mainers elected him to the U.S. Senate. Muskie was the first Democrat from Maine to hold that post in the twentieth century (1959-1980). From 1980 to 1981, he served as U.S. secretary of state.

Many great poets have come from Maine. **Henry Wadsworth Longfellow** (1807-1882) was born in Portland. He became the country's best known poet of the 1800s. Longfellow wrote "Paul Revere's Ride." This poem has been a children's favorite for nearly 150 years. He also wrote *Evangeline*, a very long poem. It told of the French Acadians who were forced to leave Canada.

Edwin Arlington Robinson (1869-1935) and **Edna St. Vincent Millay** (1892-1950) also wrote poems. Robinson was born in Head Tide. "Miniver Cheevy" is one of his best-known poems. He was the first poet to win a Pulitzer Prize. Altogether he won three Pulitzers (1922, 1925, 1928). Millay was born in Rockland. Her poems captured the rebellious feelings of young people. She won the 1923 Pulitzer Prize in poetry.

Sarah Orne Jewett (1849-1909) was born in South Berwick. Her father was a country doctor. Sarah went with him as he visited patients. She grew

Edwin Arlington Robinson

to love small-town Mainers. Later, she wrote stories about them. *The Country of the Pointed Firs* is Jewett's most famous novel.

Kate Douglas Wiggin (1856-1923) was born in Pennsylvania. She spent many summers in Hollis, Maine. Wiggin became a teacher. In 1878, she helped found the first kindergartens on the West Coast. Later, she became a famous children's author. *Rebecca of Sunnybrook Farm* is a well-known Kate Douglas Wiggin novel.

The Stanley twins were born in Kingfield. **Francis Stanley** (1849-1918) became a photographer. **Freelan Stanley** (1849-1940) became a high school principal. The twins were also inventors. In 1897, they created the Stanley Steamer. It was an early automobile.

John Ford (1895-1973) was born in Portland. In 1917, he began directing movies. Ford is the

Left to right: Kate Douglas Wiggin, John Ford, Sarah Orne Jewett

only director to win four Academy Awards. They were for *The Informer* (1935), *The Grapes of Wrath* (1940), *How Green Was My Valley* (1941), and *The Quiet Man* (1952).

Many people love being scared—in stories and movies. A Mainer is a master of scary stories. **Stephen King** was born in Portland in 1947. As a child, he made up stories. The hero in them was "Cannonball Cannon." Later, King became famous for such books as *Carrie* and *Firestarter*. Many of his tales have become movies.

Joan Benoit Samuelson was born in Portland in 1957. While in high school, she broke her leg skiing. To get back in shape, she began running. Joan Benoit Samuelson became a great long-distance runner. She trained by running more than 100 miles a week. In 1984, she won an Olympic gold medal. It was for the first Olympic women's marathon race.

Samantha Smith (1972-1985) was born in Augusta. In 1983, she wrote to a Russian leader. Samantha shared with him her fear of war with his country. The Russians invited Samantha to visit them. Her trip helped bring the United States and Russia closer together. In 1985, Samantha died in a plane crash. Later, Mount Samantha Smith in Russia was named for her. It stands 13,000 feet tall.

A marathon race covers 26 miles, 385 yards.

The birthplace of Samantha Smith, Henry Wadsworth Longfellow, Margaret Chase Smith, and Hannibal Hamlin . . .

Home also to Winslow Homer, Kate Douglas Wiggin, and James G. Blaine . . .

The state that gave us earmuffs, the blackboard, and chewing gum . . .

The country's top producer of lobsters and blueberries . . .

This is Maine—the Pine Tree State!

Samantha Smith, with the letter she received from Soviet Premier Yuri Andropov

Did You Know?

Maine makes more toothpicks than any other state. The Pine Tree State produces 50 billion toothpicks a year. That is ten for each person on earth.

The Maine coon cat is the state's official cat. This cat looks a little like a raccoon. Maine coon cats can grow to be 30 pounds. They are the biggest pet cats.

Although Maine is up north, it is sometimes called Down East. New England sailors headed downwind (with the wind) when traveling east along Maine's coast. *Down* **from** *downwind* **was combined with** *east* **to make the term** *Down East.* **Mainers are sometimes called** *Down-Easters.*

A clipper ship built at Rockland set a sailing record in 1854. The *Red Jacket* crossed the Atlantic Ocean in only thirteen days.

A native of Limerick, Maine, created one of the first children's library departments. Anne Carroll Moore (1871-1961) did this while working as a librarian in New York.

Kate Douglas Wiggin's book *Rebecca of Sunnybrook Farm* **was made into several movies. One version starred Shirley Temple.**

The country's largest yellow birch tree is at Deer Isle, Maine. Its trunk is 21 feet around. A 93-foot-tall tree at Hartford, Maine, is the country's largest paper birch.

In 1906, one of the Stanley twins' cars traveled a record 130 miles per hour.

On July 4, 1866, a boy playing with fireworks started a fire in Portland. No one was killed, but the fire destroyed half the city.

Peekaboo Mountain is in eastern Maine.

Morganite is a reddish gemstone. The world's largest morganite crystal was found in Maine in 1989. It weighed 80 pounds.

Maine has towns named Bald Head, Christmas Cove, Robinhood, Owls Head, and Bingo.

Union holds its Blueberry Festival each August. A Blueberry Queen is chosen. There is a blueberry pancake breakfast and a blueberry-pie-baking contest. The children's blueberry-pie-eating contest is a highlight of the festival. The three children who eat the most blueberry pie in a given time win prizes.

Maine is the only state with just one syllable in its name.

Maine is famous for lobsters, clams, and blueberries. Mainers make lobster stew, lobster salad, and lobster baked in seaweed. They make "Maine clam chowder" with potatoes and clams. "Clamburgers" are shaped like hamburgers. But they are made with chopped clams. Mainers put blueberries in pancakes, pudding, and muffins. Blueberry pie is a favorite Maine dessert.

The University of Maine won the 1993 college hockey title.

MAINE INFORMATION

State flag

White pine cones

Chickadee

Area: 33,215 square miles (thirty-ninth among the states in size)

Greatest Distance North to South: 320 miles

Greatest Distance East to West: 210 miles

Borders: New Hampshire on the west; Canada to the east, north, and northwest; the Atlantic Ocean to the south and east

Highest Point: Mount Katahdin, 5,267 feet above sea level

Lowest Point: Sea level, along the Atlantic Ocean

Hottest Recorded Temperature: 105° F. (at North Bridgton, on July 10, 1911)

Coldest Recorded Temperature: -48° F. (at Van Buren, on January 19, 1925)

Statehood: The twenty-third state, on March 15, 1820

Origin of Name: Some say English explorers coined *Maine,* which was short for *Mainland;* others say the area was named for a part of France called *Maine*

Capital: Augusta (since 1832)

Previous Capital: Portland (1820-1832)

Counties: 16

United States Senators: 2

United States Representatives: 2 (as of 1992)

State Senators: 35

State Representatives: 151

State Song: "State of Maine Song," by Roger Vinton Snow

State Motto: *Dirigo* (Latin, meaning "I lead")

Nicknames: "Pine Tree State," "Down East"

State Seal: Adopted in 1820

State Flag: Adopted in 1909

State Flower: White pine cone and tassel

State Bird: Chickadee

State Tree: White pine

State Animal: Moose

State Cat: Maine coon cat

State Fish: Landlocked salmon

State Insect: Honeybee

Some Rivers: Androscoggin, Kennebec, Penobscot, Machias, Piscataquis, Aroostook, Allagash, St. John, St. Croix

Some Lakes: Moosehead, Belgrade Lakes, Grand Lakes, Rangeley, Sebago

Some Islands: Mount Desert, Vinalhaven, Monhegan, Great Wass, Isle au Haut

Wildlife: Moose, black bears, white-tailed deer, bobcats, coyotes, foxes, beavers, lynxes, martens, minks, skunks, rabbits, squirrels, harbor seals, whales, sea gulls, puffins, chickadees, ducks, many other kinds of birds, brook trout, landlocked salmon, bass, perch, cod, flounder, tuna, many other kinds of fish

Manufactured Products: Paper, cardboard, toothpicks, clothespins, lumber and many other wood products, shoes, clothing, boats and ships, computers, Christmas trees, packaged foods

Farm Products: Potatoes, blueberries, peas, dry beans, apples, milk, eggs, beef cattle, oats, strawberries, raspberries, cranberries

Mining Products: Sand and gravel, limestone, clay, garnets, peat

Population: 1,227,928, thirty-eighth among the states (1990 U.S. Census Bureau figures)

Major Cities (1990 Census):

Portland	64,358	Augusta	21,325
Lewiston	39,757	Biddeford	20,710
Bangor	33,181	Waterville	17,173
Auburn	24,309	Westbrook	16,121
South Portland	23,163	Saco	15,181

White pines

Puffin

Maine History

In 1690, Mainer William Phipps defeated the French in Canada.

8000 B.C.—The first people, the ancestors of the American Indians, reach Maine

3000-1000 B.C.—Maritime Indians leave huge mounds made of oyster shells

1497-99—John Cabot explores Maine's coast and claims the land for England

1524—Giovanni da Verrazano explores Maine's coast and claims it for France

1623—The first successful English settlement in Maine is begun at Saco

1629—The English government gives Maine to Ferdinando Gorges

1631—Settlers build Maine's first sawmill and begin exporting lumber

1632—Portland is begun as Falmouth

1652—Maine comes under Massachusetts' control

1677—Massachusetts buys Maine for about $6,000 from the Gorges family

1689-1763—France and England fight several wars for control of North America

1763—England wins control of North America from France

1775-83—Americans fight for independence from England

1775—Mainers capture the English ship *Margaretta* at Machias in the first sea battle of the Revolutionary War

1783—The United States wins its independence from England

1785—Maine's first newspaper, the *Falmouth Gazette,* is begun in present-day Portland

1816—The weather is so cold that Mainers call this year "eighteen-hundred-and-froze-to-death"

1820—Maine becomes the twenty-third state on March 15

1826—John Russwurm of Bowdoin College becomes one of the country's first black college graduates

1832—Augusta becomes Maine's permanent capital

1834—The Maine Antislavery Society is formed at Augusta

1860—Hannibal Hamlin of Maine is elected vice president of the United States

1866—On July 4, a fire destroys half of Portland, causing over $6 million in damages

1894—Completion of the Aroostook Railroad helps Maine farmers ship potatoes to other states

1898—The Spanish-American War begins after the battleship *Maine* is blown up in Havana, Cuba; about 2,000 Mainers serve in the war

1917-18—After the United States enters World War I, more that 35,000 Mainers serve

1929-39—During the Great Depression many Maine farms, factories, and banks fail

1939-45—After the United States enters World War II, about 95,000 Mainers serve; about 2,000 give their lives

1948—Mainer Margaret Chase Smith becomes the first woman elected to the U.S. Senate

1958—Edmund Muskie becomes the first Democrat in the twentieth century elected by Maine to the U.S. Senate

1980—The U.S. government agrees to pay $81.5 million to the Penobscot and Passamaquoddy Indians for land wrongly seized; Edmund Muskie becomes secretary of state for President Jimmy Carter

1989—Mainer George Mitchell becomes majority leader of the U.S. Senate

1994—Angus King is elected governor

1995—The Portsmouth Naval Shipyard is taken off the government's list of base closures because it is the only shipyard in the Northeast with the ability to service nuclear submarines

Vice President Hannibal Hamlin

MAP KEY

GLOSSARY

ancestor: A person from whom one is descended, such as a grandfather or great-grandmother

ancient: Relating to a time early in history

antislavery: Against slavery

billion: A thousand million (1,000,000,000)

capital: A city that is the seat of government

capitol: The building in which the government meets

climate: The typical weather of a place

coast: The land along a large body of water

colony: A settlement outside a parent country but ruled by the parent country

depression: A period of very hard times with widespread joblessness

estuary: An arm of the ocean located at the mouth of a river

explorer: A person who visits and studies unknown lands

glacier: A mass of slowly moving ice

light: A short way of referring to a lighthouse

million: A thousand thousand (1,000,000)

patriot: A person who loves and supports his or her country

permanent: Lasting

pollute: To make dirty

population: The number of people in a place

recession: A period of hard times that is less severe than a depression

refuge: A safe place

slavery: A practice in which some people are owned by other people

sleigh: A vehicle, usually pulled by horses, that is used for traveling over snow

tourism: The business of providing such services as food and lodging for travelers

transportation: Moving goods or people by using ships, trains, airplanes, or cars

unemployment: A lack of jobs

Two of Maine's lovely coastal towns are New Harbor (left) and Camden (right).

PICTURE ACKNOWLEDGMENTS

Front cover, © Steve Terrill; 1, © Steve Terrill; 2, Tom Dunnington; 3, © Jim Scourletis; 5, Tom Dunnington; 6-7, © Steve Terrill; 8, © Steve Terrill; 9 (left), © Steve Terrill; 9 (right), Courtesy of Hammond, Incorporated, Maplewood, New Jersey; 10, © Lynn M. Stone; 11, © T. Algire/H. Armstrong Roberts; 12, Courtesy of the Maine Maritime Museum; 14, North Wind Picture Archives, hand-colored; 15, North Wind Picture Archives, hand-colored; 17 (top), Stock Montage, Inc.; 17 (bottom), North Wind Picture Archives, hand-colored; 18, © North Wind Pictures; 19, North Wind Picture Archives, hand-colored; 20, © David L. Brown/Tom Stack & Associates; 22 (left), Sophia Smith Collection, Smith College, Northampton, Massachusetts; 22 (right), North Wind Picture Archives; 23, Collections of the Maine Historical Society; 24, © Tony Stone Images; 25, Courtesy of the Maine Maritime Museum; 26 (both pictures), Courtesy of the Maine Maritime Museum; 27, © Photri, Inc.; 28, © Kevin Shields/N E Stock Photo; 29, © Kevin Shields/N E Stock Photo; 30, © Kevin Shields/N E Stock Photo; 31 (top), © North Wind Pictures; 31 (bottom), © Clyde H. Smith/N E Stock Photo; 32 (both pictures), © Kip Brundage/N E Stock Photo; 33, © Glen Allison/Tony Stone Images; 34-35, © Tom Algire/H. Armstrong Roberts; 36, © Thomas H. Mitchell/N E Stock Photo; 37 (left), © N. Dunham/H. Armstrong Roberts; 37 (right), © Steve Terrill; 38 (top), © Grover Photography/N E Stock Photo; 38 (bottom), © Kevin Shields/N E Stock Photo; 39, © James Blank/Root Resources; 40 (left), © Tom Till; 40 (right), © T. Algire/H. Armstrong Roberts; 41, © Mark Sisco/Root Resources; 42, © Frank Siteman/mga/Photri; 43, © Mark Sisco/Root Resources; 45, © Kevin Shields/N E Stock Photo; 46, Stock Montage, Inc.; 47 (both pictures), Stock Montage, Inc.; 48, AP PhotoColor; 49, AP/Wide World Photos; 50, AP/Wide World Photos; 51 (left), Dictionary of American Portraits; 51 (right), AP/Wide World Photos; 53, AP/Wide World Photos; 54, Courtesy of the Mariners' Museum, Newport News, Virginia; 55 (top), © *Automobile Quarterly;* 55 (bottom), © Mark Segal/Tony Stone Images; 56 (top), Courtesy Flag Research Center, Winchester, Massachusetts 01890; 56 (middle), © Jerry Hennen; 56 (bottom), © Skip Moody/Dembinsky Photo Assoc.; 57 (top), © Kitty Kohout/Root Resources; 57 (bottom), © Camerique/H. Armstrong Roberts; 58, Stock Montage, Inc.; 59, Dictionary of American Portraits; 60, Tom Dunnington; 62 (left), © H. Armstrong Roberts; 62 (right), © Gene Ahrens; back cover, © Tom Algire Photography/Tom Stack & Associates

INDEX

Page numbers in boldface type indicate illustrations.

ABOUT THE AUTHOR

Dennis Brindell Fradin is the author of 150 published children's books. His works for Childrens Press include the Young People's Stories of Our States series, the Disaster! series, and the Thirteen Colonies series. Dennis is married to Judith Bloom Fradin, who taught high-school and college English for many years. She is now Dennis's chief researcher. The Fradins are the parents of two sons, Anthony and Michael, and a daughter, Diana. Dennis graduated from Northwestern University in 1967 with a B.A. in creative writing, and has lived in Evanston, Illinois, since that year.